www.gamesyouloved.com
@gamesyouloved
www.facebook.com/gamesyouloved
www.youtube.com/gamesyouloved

Your daily dose of retro gaming, relive those memories!
BLOG - VIDEO - TWITTERFEED - ARTICLES

@RGDSpodcast
www.facebook.com/RGDSshow
RSS: http://retrogamingdailyshow.libsyn.com
iTunes

A podcast about retro gaming by retro gamers

A note to my fellow retro gamers.

Firstly, I'd like to say a big thank you for paying an interest in this snippet of my gaming memories. Hopefully a walk down memory lane with me will bring a smile to your face. Rather than bombarding you, the reader, with technical jargon I wanted this small book to take you back in time so I have explored on paper my sentimentality and personal memories.

The seed of the idea came from my writing for www.GamesYouLoved.com and the time I spend hosting the RGDS podcast. An acoustic guitarist and singer-songwriter by trade, I'm an avid fan of retro gaming, a lover of the seaside, a full time day-dreamer and a grower of an autumnal beard.

Welcome to my brain box...

Andy

CONTENTS

06: Memories Of A Retro Gamer

12: Commodore Format

16: Megadrive 32X

20: Polygon Dreams

24: Dizzy

26: Classic Tunes

30: Sinclair Spectrum +2 128K

34: Nintendo Gameboy

38: LCD Handhelds in the 80's

40: Donkey Kong Country

44: Arcades & Crashing Waves

47: Bring Ya Friends!

48: Sega Saturn

52: Panic Attacks & Retro Life Hacks

MEGA DRIVE AND MEGA-CD GAMING FROM THE UK, USA AND JAPAN

MEGA

NOVEMBER £2.50

C & KNUCKLES
USIVE PLUG-THRU
REVIEW

AND KNUCKLES DOOMSDAY ZONE REVEALED INSIDE
URING EARTHWORM JIM, LION KING, MM2 AND MORE

A RETRO GAMER

A large glow flickers around a dark room, curtains drawn, a wet drizzly winter night outside and a dark grey box sits to my left. I'm sat on a bunk bed with 80's décor around me in a box room that most young kids were ushered into in modest family homes. My friend and neighbour was lucky enough to have an actual computer with colour TV and I was allowed round there (as long as I was back by 8.30pm).

Pacmania was one of my first memories of being immersed in a new world running off of the futuristic and beautifully designed ZX Spectrum +2 128k. I loved everything about it, the clunky tape buttons, the screeching loading screens and bright psychedelic block colours that made new fantasy worlds come to life. I would do anything to get round there and play it... so it didn't do any harm to my fascination when a Nintendo Entertainment System was acquired by him just months later...

Supermario Bros was, and still is, so many peoples entry point into gaming. Everything about the game is beautifully designed, the controls are weighted perfectly as is the sound, the cartoony graphics and the atmospheres between each level. I was hooked in all things Mario. I got the McDonald's figures, Game and Watch games, wrist watch games and loved the cartoon, but still the NES was out of my price point and far too much money to ask my Dad for. I needed an excuse, something that would maybe benefit me in the future...

I became something of a computer wiz kid at school, I'd learn about things from simple kids style books and read magazines to learn even more. Some things I even understood, and I started to know my RAM's from my ROM's by using the BBC Micro Computers at school. Then another turning point came when the school got a new computer... a single Acorn Archimedes 3000; the machine looked like it could run the pentagon! I watched my first video clip on a school computer as the class gathered round cross legged on the floor looking up at the screen in wonder. I forget what encyclopaedia it was maybe Encarta or Britannica, but Neil Armstrong's moon speech was viewed in grainy full motion video. It was absolutely transfixing and I couldn't believe the data that was being displayed on this computer in front of me, this was something for the TV programme Tomorrow's World!

Systems I have owned:

Commodore 64
Nintendo Gameboy
Sega Master System 2
Sega Megadrive
Sega 32X
Sega Saturn
Nintendo 64
XBOX

XBOX 360
Sony PS2
Gameboy Advance SP
Sega Dreamcast
Nintendo Wii
Amstrad CPC 464
Nintendo DS
Various LCD handheld games

486 PC
(for Duke Nukem & Doom)
Various PC's
IOS

It seemed all my friends around me were getting home computers in the late 80's. Even the working class had them now, it wasn't just the few who had the office 'study' containing a 486 PC with Prince Of Persia or Wing Commander being its only games, it was now common place for a house hold to have an Amiga, Atari ST, Commodore 64 or maybe even the Sega Megadrive! I was looking for something to fall in love with, something that could teach me but offer the games and back catalogue of software. This is when after playing the Dizzy franchise, using the keyboard and immersing myself in Commodore Format I fell in love with the C64.

My Dad was possibly convinced in getting me a computer once he knew it wasn't a fad and the C64 had a keyboard. It justified its purchase and although I maybe came into the 8bit game rather late as the Amiga was already out and growing, my acquisition of this well-loved home computer was something of a wonder to me. I had the "Playful Intelligence" system pack with the game cartridge including Flimbos Quest, Fiendish Freddies Big Top'O'Fun, Klax and International Soccer.

I bought the Adventures of Dizzy game pack straight away and from then on collected everything the Oliver Twins did (Steg the Slug is an underrated classic). I was an avid reader of both Commodore Format and ZZap 64 and saved my pocket money to buy budget games (but not full price, they were sometimes £12!). The cover mount tapes were my way into the software which was a perfect balance of old classics for free and new demos. This was something us 8bit computer nerds had over the console junkies... free games each month.

It's so hard to explain the memories I have with the C64 and the Sega Megadrive without sounding slightly mad. For me the Commodore opened up my head to a world of fantasy and imagination. It gives me a warm safe glow inside when I think about myself before going into my teens properly where nothing else mattered but the games and the vibe of the software. It got me at a time when nothing is expected of you and you can fully connect with the games and their secret worlds.

Maybe that's the magic I tap into each time I play something from the 8 and 16bit era and maybe even the N64.... A childlike view on the world before the realisation of responsibility and work. Or maybe it's just something simpler, a way of entertaining an inquisitive mind that likes to be manipulated in fantasy lands... I think it's a bit of all these things! One things for sure, when I hear the opening music of Cyberdyne Warrior on the C64 I still feel invincible!
After the 16bit generation things got real! The scrap to the top in the Playstation era was undoubtedly exciting, and I was a great age for it. Seeing the Jaguar, Saturn, 32X, Amiga 32, Playstation, 3DO, Neo Geo, and more emerge was fascinating and exciting as games started to cross over into proper mainstream life. Some would argue it was mainstream before but there was still a stigma attached to gaming in the media and the playground.

The Playstation tapped into the come-down 90's generation and made playing Wipe-Out after clubbing cool. Games were no longer an exclusive club, everyone had them (and only ever talked about FIFA or Call Of Duty!). My proper devotion to new gaming died at the PS2, as that was the generation when I stopped buying magazines and looking online for new information. I didn't mind at that point as I was well and truly consumed with music and in the process of working up to playing my songs in front of people; I still enjoyed playing my old games.

I have owned and loved all things Sega Megadrive (including the hated Mega CD & 32X), Gameboy, N64, Dreamcast, SNES, Gameboy Advance, PS2, XBOX 360 & Wii and many more. My love for games is now going backwards as I'm now a professional musician so I don't have the time or the inclination to immerse myself in the new Assassin's Creed. You can't just pick up and play anymore, everything is so massive, big budget, and complicated with online achievements, downloadables etc. I connect every now and then but I much prefer picking up the Game Boy Advance and killing an hour by entering an old world.

For me, gaming should be about escapism. Yes, it REALLY is all about escapism… escapism is a beautiful drug that will never leave me and one which I have now transported over in connecting with people onstage through my music. When I reflect on my childhood gaming memories there will always be an element of rose tinted glasses, sure, but it's great to reconnect with that naive childlike simplicity when everything was easy and without responsibility.

Back in the day, gamers were seen as geeky, weedy and the underdogs, but to me they were the people who let the fantasy wash over them and wanted to shut the world out because at times it was boring! They were the true heroes… I loved the outside world and spent so much time as a kid appreciating it, but my imagination was so vivid and overflowing that games were my outlet to control that before I found the acoustic guitar.

I still love to switch off the world and defend the galaxy from an alien horde, collect gold coins, find power ups and see what's on the next screen…

Green mushroom anyone?!

Commodore

MEMORIES OF...

COMMODORE FORMAT

A solitary BBC Microcomputer sat un-used in a huge trolley of ridiculously exaggerated self-importance. All its cables hung down like a deflated octopus over a huge metal frame that should have been used to build a new structure of some kind or perhaps to house a delicate bomb experiment from the 1940's!

Why schools in the 80's wheeled their BBC's around in this massive frame still baffles me to this day but it did spark something in me that I didn't quite harness until later on; Chuckie Egg, Frogger, and a text adventure, that I don't remember, began to trigger an interest.

This interest was compounded during a rainy winter in the late 80's when there was nothing to do but push a tape copy of Pacmania into the built in datassette of the ZX Spectrum +2. But, aside from the machine's beautiful looks, there was something coming that would make me obsessed with all things Commodore.

Allow me to introduce you to a friend of mine (you won't know him) his name is Ashley Penny. He's not famous now, unless you count a really quick completion of Fantasy Land Dizzy for celebrity status! Back in the day he was a small lad who looked like he was made from porcelain (he did actually break his arm by getting a Shoot 5 kicked at him!) and seemed to be leagues ahead of me in computer knowledge. As you'll remember, at aged nine or ten, sleep-overs are popular and by their very nature introduce to you completely new households and family cultures… and this was the ultimate.

Ashley asked me to come round and play computer - he didn't say what it was! I arrived to find he had a C64C with the Dizzy Collection. From the moment I saw the start-up screen, the font, the contours on the slightly creamed machine, the separate datasette and the white annihilator joystick with the red buttons, I felt that everything about it seemed classier than the Spectrum. That evening I'd come across a Commodore Format that was lying on the floor open on a Dizzy map and I wanted in. That was it. That's what I wanted to start my computer career ladder and convincing my Dad to get me the Playful Intelligence pack was actually easier than I thought. Maybe he thought I was going to learn code?! I've tried a few code listings from CF over the years but other than that I was never going to be the next Public Domain hero by any means.

After the acquisition of this great machine it was obvious where I was going to go for my C64 literature... the magazine that I picked up from the floor that night and my love for Commodore Format was born. The first edition I remember getting through was issue 12, the Speedball 2 cover and demo. On the Covertape was Rodland, PP Hammer, and Speedball 2 (which I personally think is better than the 16bit versions although I'm aware I'm probably alone on that fact). The magazine had serious reviews with a sense of humour that even a kid could understand, BUT I was aware that aspects of the writing were going over my head. Basically, it was universal with a wide range appeal, clear bold presentation and wasn't trying to be too cool all the time like ZZAP64!

I got both mags when I could and enjoyed both, however CF always held that top spot for me as it came across a little more classy and concise. I have so many memories of this magazine mostly of its monthly glow of warmth; and I know that's a hard thing to explain to someone who doesn't have an obsessive nature like myself! When I get into something I live it, and this was no exception. It became a Bible that I took everywhere with me and the Covertapes became my window to the C64 world. The Covertapes alone were worth the asking price as the full games were nearly always classics and the demos were exclusives and never a cop out. You normally got a full level to play or a good chance to sample the game or, like me, if you couldn't afford the full game then you could play the cover tapes all month until you could afford a budget game; recommended by Roger Frames of course!

One of my favourite issues by far is the Elvira front cover issue 15, it encapsulates everything about being an early teenager to me and it was also a great time for the mag. I was into zombies, having somewhat of a penchant for the undead, so getting introduced to the gorgeous creepy looking Elvira was quite something for a confused teenager... needless to say the poster went straight on my wall! That issue had everything: a round-up of driving games, reviews of PP Hammer, Smash TV, Elvira, the Clyde Guide, and a map of Aliens.

Other favourite issues included 20, with the Space Crusade cover. Its Covertape containing Catalypse and Bod the Alien were exceptional. I played issue 22's Robocod and DJ Puff over and over again and special mentions go to UGH!, Fuzzball, Arnie, Addams Family, Cyberdyne Warrior, Demon Blue and Firelord.

Issue 17's Covertape was also probably the most complete for me which leads me ask… Who compiled these classic covertapes? Surely whoever was in control of this held the keys to potential success of games across the country? Everybody's access to the games before the internet was through this media so they had quite the power back then! Like I said earlier, I loved the writing of CF and the presentation deserved its own "It's a Corker!" accolade. I really liked when ZAPP64! became Commodore Force the writing style was more coherent to me; I'm sure, as being quite a devout bunch, the ZAPP fans will hate me for that! I loved all mags on the humble C64 who was starting to really strain under the weight by now and even I had a Gameboy and Megadrive running alongside it. It still didn't stop me getting CF though and as I watched it limp out of print a part of my childhood innocence went with it (by now I'd discovered girls, guitars, music, and I wanted to express myself in different ways).

I got rid of all my issues in the late 90's in a weird exorcism routine to try and start a new, partly because I was always getting told I was a hoarder and also to try and reinvent myself as someone who didn't need kids mags… I've always regretted it… they were never kids mags… they were little snapshots of what growing up with a new technology was about and a large part of who I am. When I was asked to do this small piece for a great resource and pool of nostalgia - commodoreformat.wordpress.com - it really made me feel eleven again. I wrote in to this mag several times (I physically wrote as well, it was the 90's!) and never got in, so this opportunity felt like redemption! I love writing about retro games now and hope to continue to do so. I want to do my bit in keeping the dream of institutes like Commodore Format alive. Lying on the floor of a 70's styled backroom playing Flimbos' Quest through a beaten up old Matsui colour TV on silent whilst your Dad watches the proper TV, (probably Noel's House Party or Strike It Lucky) will never be recreated once you lose your innocence. Writing like this brings it back a little…

MEGADRIVE 32X

I wanted it to work… I whipped myself up into a frenzy of expectation literally trying to will it to fly into success, much like the Lee Evans comedic idea of how a plane takes off using the passengers' will alone. Deep down I knew it wasn't going to work, yet always being attracted to the underdog I loyally went down with the ship believing Sega wasn't going to let the death of the 32X go without realising its potential. It's easy to see why it was an attractive proposition; the prices alone of the new-fangled 32bit hardware were completely unreachable to a boy with a paper round and only a Xmas present dream. Here was an option using an upgrade to my existing console the Megadrive 2 that sat under my TV and I too could be a member of the 32bit world. Especially as my Dad got it for me nearly a year after its release second hand for around £40!

I'm not going to go into the technical aspect too much as it's well documented as being considered the beginning of Sega's fall into the precipice of hardware history. For me the 32X symbolises a missed opportunity, Sega's incredible thirst in hardware development ideas and also the company's madness that encapsulates its spirit. Sega's colours are black (yes I understand the grey and white Japanese colours) and to me they have always been concerned with the daring, the grungy, the mad and the gritty. Nintendo were always well organised, slightly cold in its business approach, a sign of the upmost quality and family friendly. With this in mind I adore Sega's mental approach to the early 90's. It got cocky and spewed out all these mad ideas throwing money at all of them like an excited rich teenager. I love them for that and I love the 32X and all its hated foibles. Through the year of its release I looked at the screenshots of Doom, Star Wars Arcade and the Virtua games getting excited and thinking how great it would be to own them but secretly knowing that Sega weren't thinking quick enough in terms of the market… the PlayStation changed everything.

Everyone had a perceived rich mate. That friend. He got all the consoles on launch even at 13/14 years old with a few games to boot. When the PlayStation came out he had it straight away and round his house playing Wipeout and Ridge Racer I knew that whatever Sega had in mind for the 32X they weren't here at this level. They weren't thinking about the future of the market… they weren't really thinking at all as it all went a little Charlie & The Chocolate Factory for the early 90's.

To me even though Sega at one point were winning the war against Nintendo it always felt as though Sega were playing catch up to the power of the SNES and were kind of secretly embarrassed, hence the over aggressive posturing and incessant add-ons.

Bare in mind when the 32X came out as did Donkey Kong Country a beautiful silicon rendered platformer that looked incredible and the 32X didn't really look to me like it had anything to rival it. It did have Doom though and for some reason everyone forgets that it was generally well received over in the UK when released, time has backlashed that version with vengeance, much like Be Here Now by Oasis. The machine was actually quite powerful but didn't realise its own potential through being ridiculously hard to code; Sega confusing everybody by releasing the Saturn so soon afterwards and generally being too late for anyone to actually grasp exactly what it was! This is all with hindsight though. No-one knew at this point what Sony were going to achieve.

Games like Virtua Fighter, Virtua Racing, Stellar Assault, Darxide, and Star Wars Arcade are all very competent games that have maybe not aged well because they are the start of 3D gaming but were very exiting at the time. NBA Jam TE, Tempo, Mortal Kombat 2, NFL Quarterback Club also have interesting scaling and rotation tricks. I never really was sold on the apparent arcade perfect conversions of Space Harrier and Afterburner, but maybe that was because to me I had used all my love for them games 6 years previous! I had a strange love affair with Metal Head because it was trying to do something spectacular even though it ran at a snail's pace, and Motocross Championship was meant to be a texture mapped dream but ended up a dirty mess, but for some reason I love it and still do today!

I also adored the graphic design of the box art, the cardboard sleeves and cartridges and the cardboard nest the cartridges sat in. Like many of Sega's advertising campaigns after the very successful Megadrive ones, the 32X ads were bizarre to say the least lacking continuity and flare, failing to capture the imagination of the gaming public and seeming to consist mostly of sexual connotations and innuendo.

If the 32X had been instead of the Mega CD we may now be hailing its presence over gaming. 3D manipulation abilities bolted onto the most popular console of the time? Nintendo would have had to bolt on the SFX chip at every given opportunity as the future was definitely 3D polygonal graphics. The 32X wasn't quite there but not a million miles away from the Saturn in its inside architecture but obviously not as powerful. With this in mind if the add-on had been released to a wide eyed, arcade hungry audience of 1992/93, Virtua Fighter alone could have been enough for the machine to gather speed and realise its potential. This would have meant we would have had the games that were threatening to come out for the machine.

Titles such as Virtual Hamster, Daytona (hopefully with a good framerate), Shadow Of Atlantis, Rayman, Beyond Zero Tolerance, Soul Star X, Ecco The Dolphin, Bug!, Alone In The Dark 2, and Alien Trilogy which later appeared on the Saturn. This could have helped make the machine slot into the consciousness of the public and for them to trust it more. Essentially this is what Sega lost in the gaming public...their trust. It was far too late considering what the PlayStation was offering with its textured polygons and high framerate, people wanted in. The Saturn was also damaged because of Sega's confusion but its legacy with gamers has been intact due to its excellent games something that the 32X didn't have many of.

Much has been made of the faults of the 32X but I don't think that much of them would be talked about now if it was a success. Connecting the unit was annoying because of the huge plug transformers but who was moving it about all the time? I did it once and then it stayed there...being a working 32X!... I never understood what the fuss was about? Physical hardware expansions rarely worked in gaming hardware history but I don't think this failure was down to a plug issue, Sega just rushed this whole idea and we wouldn't be talking about plugs, connectors, metal plates, or its mushroom shape had it all been a success. With this in mind it does irk me somewhat to see every YouTube video of the machine ranting on about its connection woes. I didn't know anyone that didn't have a spaghetti junction of cables behind their TV in the 90's and a 32X wouldn't have really been a problem. Saying that, how lovely was it when the PlayStation 2 came along and you had your DVD player, CD player and gaming machine with one plug and your TV!

Basically, it seems everybody took their eye off the ball allowing Sony to demolish everyone. The Saturn struggled to pick up pace in Europe even though nowadays it's revered as one of the best retro gaming machines. The 3DO, Jaguar, Amiga 32 etc. all crashed and burned with only Nintendo and its 64bit cartridge machine making a significant dent into the PlayStations miraculous success. Sega were far too late to the party and should have focussed on one idea instead of the Wondermega, the Mega CD, the 32X, the Saturn, the Game Gear, the Master System, the Neptune, the Nomad, the Pic, the various peripherals, the second generation of their console range, basically they saturated their own user base with bonkers ideas. The Dreamcast was an accumulation of those ideas, but again... too late. I wouldn't have had it any other way though as this was what Sega were all about, and although it's a shame they are no longer in the hardware race they left behind a legacy of innovation and ideas.

I love the 32X, and continue to always raise a smile when I see its crazy design. I still have mine and although I don't have all the boxes for things anymore I still have kept hold of the games. In fact I may get a t-shirt with the logo on the front as I like what it stands for... a big bonkers idea that tried and failed. Project Mars will forever be remembered a failure but to me it was a beacon of Sega's bizarre personality.

SEGA-AM2 Co.,LTD.

MEMORIES OF...
POLYGON DREAMS

In the early 90's arcade era, just before the huge gaming sea-change that was the 5th generation, 'polygons' were the buzzword of choice. Magazines boasted of new machines that could move thousands of shapes per second to process the new 3D worlds we would soon be enjoying. VR headsets were presented in 'Tomorrow's World' style programmes and in the arcades everyone looked like seasick idiot pirates coming up from below deck.

POLYGON noun. Pronunciation /ˈpɒlɪg(ə)n/

(GEOMETRY) a plane figure with at least three straight sides and angles, anatomically five or more.

Tron-like landscapes were depicted in the much loved Gamesmaster programme as the future of various games started to take on this very stylised look that only plain coloured shapes can represent. A clean, stylised, and instantly recognisable look that even now still feels like it resembles the future!

I had the pleasure of playing the 1000CS Cyberspace coin up machine in some sleepy seaside town, either Portsmouth or Bognor Regis - I can't remember. It made me feel sick and disorientated at first, but I didn't care as I had played it and I was going tell everyone I had played it even if they weren't interested because I was literally in a 3D world…you know…like life!
The home ports of these games at the time are often criticised and early 3D gaming as something which maybe hasn't held up well in some instances, but for me it's all part of the charm. Polygons will flicker on and off and scenery will bend and flop about like the early dodgy sets of Ramsay Street in 90s episodes of Neighbours. For me though, like colour clash and sprite collision before it, this only adds to its charm. The arcades and home video game industry were well into their journey of merging by this point and maybe the AM2 era was arguably the last hurrah of the arcades. If you'd don't include dance machines of course!

Winning Run, Lander (Zarch), Starfox, Cybermorph, Stunt Race FX, Hard Drivin, Race Drivin, are all games released at various times with un-textured polygons that have that distinct style but there's two games I wanted to talk about here... The summer of 93 was the first time I laid my eyes on the new upright arcade cab of Virtua Fighter whilst on holiday with my best chum Chris Jackson. Nothing prepared me for those fighters moving in glorious fluid 3D. Although I had seen screenshots in magazines it didn't do it justice... it's like the difference of looking at a super soaker and actually squirting someone with one! The graphic design for this game is so iconic and it had Sega's trademark high quality all over the cabinet.

As a 12 year old kid playing Dizzy and Flimbo's Quest at home on my C64 this was an otherworldly and unobtainable experience; just like all those 80's Sega cabinets preceding it were. I remember it well as not only was it my first encounter with Virtua Fighter but I also had a crush on a girl that kept coming into the arcades that week. I didn't even speak to her... not because of the games.... just because I couldn't muster the courage! Jacky would have asked her out for a coke, maybe even a two player game of space hockey, but that's why kids like me would put in £1 to play as him as he was a double 'ard Indy Car Racer and I was just a little scrat with a global hyper colour tee-shirt on!

It was quite something that in only 2 years I'd be playing a very good port at home on my 32x and even that was virtually out of date as soon as it arrived due to the start of textured polygons in home gaming. Things moved so fast back then it seems to have slowed down over the last 10 years; we basically get better looking versions of the same game. The breakthrough into 3D was a real eye-opener and something that I guess the Wii was trying to create with a similar sea-change into interactive motion; it wasn't quite to be though.

Virtua Fighter is a game I still play regularly on my Saturn and never seem to tire of it. I'd go as far as to say I like its vibe more than Virtua Fighter 2 but I'm aware that's potentially mad! Which brings me to one of my favourite games of all time... Virtua Racing. Released just before Fighter in 1992 by the legendary Sega AM2 this game set the bar in terms of racers for years to come. The different camera angles, smooth framerate and gorgeous visuals set it apart from anything at the time and things moved so quickly after that with Daytona and Sega Rally both being released very quickly afterwards complete with textured polygons. As soon as I had played it in the arcades and sat in the perfectly formed plastic formula one car, I wanted it at home instantly on the trusty Megadrive and it wasn't very long that I would have to wait.

Most people's first foray into import games was the release of Street Fighter 2 on the SNES; with Buzz Lightyear toy demand-style fighting to have the cart at home! Virtua Racing was the only time I have ever bought an import on release and nagged my Dad for the Japanese version that came with a convertor in Portsmouth's Ross Records shop (it's still there!). I adored the box art and my Dad paid a little less for the Jap version. I played it to death, I was always on it... and like most Sega racers the first track is so iconic. The fairground, the Bridge that leapt out of the screen as you past through it, the VR men in the pit lane, the checkpoint music, I could play that track on repeat for hours. Little touches like the sparks that come of the titanium tray at the back of the car, tyre skid marks that stay there, and digitised speech all add to the games charm; it's the perfect arcade racer.

The game reminds me of an innocent time, an age before girls, smoking, riding around on mopeds, making music and generally being a late-teens plonker took precedent over those simple video game pleasures. It also reminds me of Sega World in Bournemouth and friends coming round for split screen action! It really was an incredible achievement to port it to the Megadrive and I had it on the 32X also.

VR still is the future in my head... blocky flat polygons are still attractive to my eye and represent everything exciting about the early 3D world. Wireframe 3D was the beginning, graphics like my TomyTronic, but that's a different story...

MEMORIES OF...
DIZZY

So much has already been written about these games and their influence is still huge today, but here's why I love Dizzy and the Dizzy collection.

The Dizzy brand was perfection and my first entry into the 80's video game world along with Pacmania. The worlds were beautifully crafted but had a similar vibe throughout, the characters and their eccentricities were similar each time. Music, humour, puzzle solving and bizarre trippy layouts were all presented like a familiar old friend and each time a game came out it was like you were entering into a concept. It was this attention to branding that made the series so popular.

Much like a Mario or Zelda game today, Dizzy brings with it a whole plethora of connotations, cartoon psychedelia, and cutesy bizarreness. It was this ideal that brought with it a childlike wonder surrounding everything about the game which, in turn, made you care for the characters involved.

As soon as the loading lights strobed out from behind the first game's loading graphic you're entering into a world in which to immerse yourself. It wasn't an arcade blaster or fighting frenzy, it was the thinking mans' text adventure arcade game. Dizzy is arguably among the first to have expansive games that involve a bit of brain matter with a "brand" like Mario or Pac Man.

It's hard to say what my favourite Dizzy game is. At a push I'd have to say the second game in the series Treasure Island Dizzy. There's something about that genius game mechanic of the underwater snorkel and the whole vibe of the game sits perfectly with my South Coast nautical roots!

With a rage inducing inventory system and its sometimes downright weird puzzles it made you want to be "present" with the game instead of just dipping into it. Sometimes infuriating, sometimes cruel, but always charming, expansive, and beautifully crafted, that first Dizzy game on the C64 will always be my first gaming love.

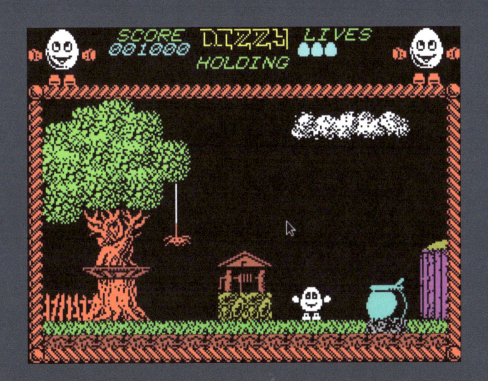

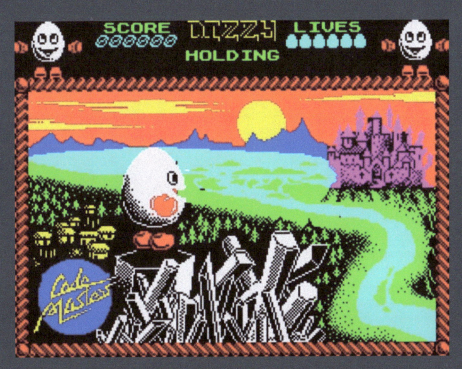

CLASSIC TUNES

Sound in video games is integral and a huge part of the experience as we all know. Sonic 'tagging' or branding (such as the sound of finding a secret in Zelda games or collecting a ring in Sonic) is so important to the in-game experience that even people who don't play retro games can easily recognise these sounds. The music in games though runs deep and although (retro games especially) have no lyrics in them they still have a huge emotional value to the players. I'm a musician now so I can't help but to have an understanding and analytical approach to how it's made. It's interesting to look back on some of my favorite themes before I knew the musicality of them and briefly analyze why I love them with hindsight, these are just a few of my favorites.

Zombies Ate My Neighbors: Main theme: SNES/Megadrive

A completely bonkers game needs a fitting soundtrack to accompany it and what makes this theme so perfect is that it draws its inspiration from the psychedelic surf/garage themes from the early 60's / late 50's that go hand in hand with the B-Movie design throughout. Perfect audio design and a classic theme, for optimum listening quality though it must be listened to whilst wearing 3D shades.

Mr Nutz: Woody Land 3 & 4: SNES

Mr Nutz although very successful across various formats never really gets talked about anymore. It has some very high production values and it's incredibly tough, maybe that's why! The music is great throughout but this particular theme perfectly captures the autumnal 'mystical forest' feel that this level evokes. The SNES's midi sounds were more complex than the Megadrives harsh dirty sonic's and none more highlighted than here. It has some odd scale choices using flat notes and slightly trippy pad sounds, the scale choices have definitely influenced my music. I tend to always have odd chords thrown into relatively standard chord progressions and this is possibly an example of why I do it.

Flimbo's Quest: Main Theme: C64

Ah the SID chip.. the lethal weapon of the C64 and those wobbly crunchy snares and basslines get the perfect outing on this cult C64 classic. Pick any tune in this game for a perfect example of the Sid in action. When someone asks for the perfect Vox amp chime I point them to early Beatles records, when someone wants to hear an example of Commodore's well-loved machine I would point them here. That level one music instantly brings me back to my youth. It's playful, fun, cutesy and quite complex for back then.

Donkey Kong Country: Aquatic Ambience: SNES

I adore Sega but for me in-house made Nintendo games always have the most incredible music. Donkey Kong Country used silicon rendering, faux 3D and some incredible musical scores to create a new experience to rival the next-gen wave coming in. The underwater level particularly gets talked about a lot with retro gamers and its ambient genius is still beautiful today. I wonder how many people let Kong or Diddy just stay idle on the sea bed because if you rushed through the level you would always miss the best bit in the musical score! Brian Eno would be proud!

Cyberdyne Warrior: Main Theme: C64

Another SID chip gem from Apex on the C64. I got this game off a powerpack from Commodore Format magazine and after loading it up left the opening screen idling because the music was so good! It has that perfect 80's drama that we came to expect from movie themes like Robocop and Terminator; the game definitely took elements from both of them. I like the looping bassline with the chords changing over the top. It's the perfect metallic arcade adventure theme that seems to be undiscovered.

Earthworm Jim: Barn Theme: N64

As we got into the 64bit era the CD based systems could hold recorded music and had game tie-in licenses like the Chemical Brothers in Wipeout. Orchestras were starting to be used to record game music but the N64 wasn't known for its sonic capabilities. Nintendo's most playable machine still sounded like Midi and sometimes even less impressive than the SNES because the N64 shared its load with the co-processor apparently! Quality isn't always the top priority when it comes to music composition though...just ask Robert Johnson! Besides its shortcomings, the N64 still made some of the best video game music in history. This redneck storming barn dance is just as whacky as the game.

Zen Intergalactic Ninja: Oil Area: Gameboy
Arcade games need drama. Contra, Streets of Rage, Golden Axe, even my favorite arcade musical passage Virtua Racing has huge drama and exaggerated musical themes. I went for this relatively unknown platformer on the Gameboy, a game that had mixed reviews that I loved back then and this theme was the perfect arcade companion to the Oil level. Listening to it now it sounds incredibly like the Street Fighter themes which as we all know are loved by everyone who owns a pad or joystick!

Mortal Kombat 2: Wastlend Theme: Megadrive
Like I said before the SNES had a more complex sound processor but sometimes the Megadrive's dirtier scuzzier sound processors made for a superior soundtrack. The SNES wasteland theme for my personal favorite Mortal Kombat game is far too clean and nice sounding. This was the version I had of the game and its aggressive, percussive call to arms is a perfect accompaniment to the violence! I love the Asian instruments making a nod to the martial arts and mystical feel the game design conjures up. Toasty!

Treasure Island Dizzy: In-game Theme: C64
I know I have two examples of the SID chip already but if you're ever feeling sad put this on YouTube, make a cup of tea, and pick up and put down items like you are Dizzy egg.

Daytona USA: Arcade/Sega Saturn
You can hear it in any arcade from half a mile away... "Dayeeetooonaaaaaaaa!" A choice for different reasons than audio excellence more for nostaglic reasons the soundtrack for Daytona is both rediculous and brilliant. So of its time that as soon as you hear it you want to play the game.

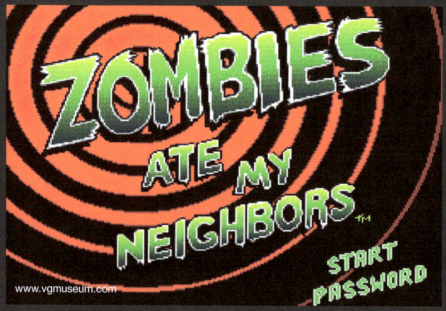

www.vgmuseum.com

28

ZX Spectrum

MEMORIES OF...

SINCLAIR SPECTRUM +2 128K

From a design point of view, I still think it's the most beautiful computer EVER made: the embossed logos, the little splash of colour on the dark or light grey finish, the Sinclair rainbow on the built-in Datacorder, chunky buttons and a LOVELY keyboard! I've never owned one. I just don't have enough room for another full-on computer; it's too big a foot-print. I'm just about maxed out under my TV of retro consoles, let alone a full on computer set-up!

I was a Commodore 64 owner and back then you had to choose sides on the age old argument Speccy or C64. I've never felt particularly tribal in life, which is possibly why I never did anything with sports as I was quite good but just wasn't arsed enough to channel a hatred of the other team/opponent. Why can't we all get along… maaaan?! Saying that, I was always a little smug inside that I'd made the right choice for my needs back then. The C64 managed to limp a little longer in the consciousness of gamers due to its game library and arcade conversion performance. The Amiga also helped the Commodore brand, although I never owned one and although the 64 was dull in colour, the graphic architecture lended itself to the late 80's and was slightly more competitive against the 8bit consoles.

I've mentioned before that my first ever experience with computers was the BBC Micros at school. The +2 signifies one of my first proper times within computing - specifically gaming. Time has been kind to the Sinclair Spectrum with hipsters and retro-heads keeping the brand alive by wearing the tee-shirts, sharing articles and lapping up anything with the extremely 80s graphic design on it. Maybe it's because it was the underdog alongside the Stateside grandness of Commodore's might or maybe it's because people remember it more fondly from their youth… or maybe it's the fact that it symbolises a very British company and figurehead in Sir Clive Sinclair; I think it's that. This brand encompasses the British underground computer game revolution in the 80s and it's all wrapped up in the connotations of what that means.

The sale of Sinclair to Amstrad in the mid 80s may make some purists shudder and if you watch films like Bedrooms to Billions you'll see that some people are so purist that as soon as people buy in droves they turn off as it becomes a unit shifting business. I experience the same in music all the time, as soon as something becomes successful the magic goes for some people and they aren't fans of that band anymore; they declare a "sell-out" if you will.

An iconic cover of the rival magazine CRASH to my ZAPP! 64 & Commodore Format from www.rediscoverthe80s.com

FEBRUARY 1984 No 1   75p

CRASH

MICRO GAMES ACTION

THE MONTHLY
SPECTRUM
SOFTWARE
REVIEW

THE BIGGEST
SPECTRUM
SOFTWARE
MAGAZINE . . .

OVER 400
GAMES
REVIEWED

TOP 20 PHONE-IN
THE CRASH HOTLINE

JOYSTICKS
BOON OR A PAIN?
& WHICH ONE TO BUY?

BEWARE THE
WRATH OF MAGRA!

SHOOT EM UP!
Invaders Galaxians - we
compare some versions

ARCADE ADVENTURE STRATEGY
SIMULATION EDUCATION UTILITIES

Become a Reviewer for CRASH!
AND WIN EXCITING SOFTWARE
in our Reviewers Competition

ENTER THE MONTHLY
CRASH QUIZ!!!
PRIZES TO BE
WON

It's a tricky argument and one which I do understand, but as I get older you realise that's just the structure of consumerism - it just doesn't mix well with art! (I'm sure most weren't complaining when they managed to buy their house with the profits of their games though!) Anyway, I digress. My point is that the +2 gets forgotten because of the sell off to Mr Apprentice and his multiple warehouses of fax machines, which I think was a mistake. Its better looking, more powerful, easier to use, still has the ethics of what Spectrum is AND had the might of Amstrad behind it... Yes, well, maybe that last one didn't quite pan out for them but in my opinion it was still a vast improvement over the rubber keyboarded gem that Sir Clive gave the world.

My experience with the machine was through a friend who was extremely spoilt by his Mother; much to my benefit of course as I got to play the +2 very frequently. Pacmania was my game of choice along with a plethora of Codemasters hits, JetPac, and Dizzy games. The graphic style has aged well because it's so distinct and psychedelic. It's bold and bright with great smooth sprites and character that only the Speccy can achieve, one which I become more endeared to as I get older. I remember the colour clash and graphical look of the spectrum looked dated compared to its competitors at the time. The advent of the Master System and the NES made the C64 look more in-line than the good'ol Speccy but its output has aged possibly better than some from the era because of how unique and clear it is and the 128K of the +2 only added to the potential of the games. The SJS - 1 Joystick was also a brilliant piece of design, looking more 80's than ED-209 from Robocop could ever muster.

I always wanted Commodore to make a C64 with the datasette built in like this as I loved how easier it was to use because of it. I had to lug my datasette around with me from my Dad's house to my Mum's house and they didn't look cool... this looked cool! Obviously, with the C64C being quite a big machine the advent of a tape machine on the side would make it comparable to a Megadrive 2/Mega CD 2 combo and who has the room for that now that we all seem to live in 2 rooms and a bathroom?!

This computer and the time in which I was graced with it, is wrapped up in all kinds of youthful memories. This is before I was ten years old maybe 1988/9 so my mind was full of very young childlike wonder and imagination... rainy streets, ghost stories, Paul Daniels Magic Show, Halloween, communicating via morse code with my mate across the street with a torch at night time from my bedroom... getting my first mountain bike (an Apollo Atomic if ya asking!), Boglins, Transformers, Ghostbusters, Fluorescent clothing, Crossbows & Catapults, walking in the mist at dusk in open fields and the ZX Spectrum +2 128K. The option screen when you turn it on always sends a shiver down the spine and I kind of don't ever want one as the memory will NEVER match the reality of it.

This legendary machine is enjoying somewhat of a renaissance at present what with the Vega, Vega + Handheld, the recreated ZX Spectrum by Elite Systems and the ZX Spectrum Next. Being a Commodore owner I obviously haven't immersed myself in the world of the Spectrum as much as I perhaps should have, but it's very special to me because it was my first proper time tinkering with the hardware and software of any computer. So, for that alone it's a huge retro gaming memory.

http://retromash.com/nash/wp-content/uploads/2014/05/Spectrum+201.jpg

Nintendo GAMEBOY

I heard a rumour in the playground that someone had brought in their Gameboy to school. I scoured the landscape like a meerkat in the desert or a submarine periscope out at sea. There was no sign of my target through the games of conkers, marbles, girls pretending they were unicorns and kids playing 5-a-side with a huge roll of socks (footballs were banned on the concrete due to previous unfortunate playtime accidents.) Then suddenly, an angelic light shone down from parted clouds around a boy and a small group of my peers; harps were playing and winged Koopas hovered above. Chiptune sonics whirled around the playground in crystal clear 3D and dot matrix sprites flew out of a tiny white box like the containment unit shut-down in Ghostbusters when all the ghosts escaped. Well, maybe I've embellished that memory, either way, his name was Matt Baker and he was now the most important lad on Earth.

I joined the huddle too and tried to get my head in the right place relative to the sunlight to see the green dot matrix screen. Eventually my turn came and I put the impeccably designed block of late 80's technology into my young hands. I loved everything about it: the blue font, the blue and red lines at the top of the grey border and the chunky red buttons (slightly rounded with a satisfying springy feel when pressed). The surface was slightly textured and one corner by the speaker being slightly rounded felt good and looked even better. It was a perfect design and still to this day (I have my original!) I think it's such a perfect and iconic piece of design. It may be big and cumbersome now but although I do like the DS, it doesn't even come close to the original in terms of aesthetics.

There was something mythical about Nintendo back then, the way they presented themselves was so coherent and concise. After playing Super Mario Brothers on the iconic NES I was obsessed with Nintendo products and bought heavily into the Mario franchise even without owning anything that could run it. I had a Mario 3 watch, the blue Mario Game & Watch game and much various merchandise. When the GameBoy was released I fell in love with it instantly. I craved one even though I loved my C64C, I wanted portable power and to be part of the Nintendo world.

I kept seeing it on telly, those two iconic ads... the 'Now you're playing with portable power' and the perfect collage collection of pop art style nuttiness that was full of culture references. Genius marketing that helped to make the system the most desirable piece of kit. The games I remember from my first encounter with Nintendo's GameBoy are Nintendo World Cup, Tetris (obviously!) and Super Mario Land but this was just the beginning of my journey through the system.

The box art was incredible for the games and being a sucker for graphic design and presentation I loved the cardboard boxes with the GameBoy logo on a metallic background as a standard. Continuity through everything is paramount in marketing and, of course, this was no exception. I could go on forever about the games but that's for another time as it gives me endless opportunity to write about the machine, so for now, my two favourites: Zelda Links Awakening and Super Mario Land 2 6 Golden Coins. Zelda Links Awakening is in my opinion the best Zelda game... (a collective "Oooooooo!" is heard across the gaming world, I'm being controversial, I know!) and I remember when Super Mario Land 2 6 Golden Coins came out and buzzed my school! Huge sprites filled the screen with SNES-like animation and imaginative enemies, worlds, level design, handling and its kooky psychedelic feel all make it captivating to me and I still play it every other month.

We all know there were drawbacks... you often couldn't see the screen in the slightest of light changes and the contrast wheel rarely compensated. The add-ons for the machine made it look like the International Space Station and made it even less portable... almost like a dog trying to get through a doorway with a piece of wood bigger than the door frame! You really needed a carry case or a good pair of combat trousers as it's maybe not Atari Lynx big but, it definitely wasn't Nokia 3210 small!

The GameBoy's legacy in the industry is one that will never fade, it was genius. Executed perfectly by a company who pioneered gaming on the move. The cynic would say it sparked times of kids putting down their marbles and conkers and watching screens, but what fun it was delving into those dot matrix worlds! Is there anything that sparks nostalgia better than those two Nintendo notes that ping out when you switch it on?!

MEMORIES OF...

LCD HANDHELDS IN THE 80's

I didn't have my first computer until my 12th birthday in 1992, the mighty C64C. I'd played many before then of course, but the cheaper option and substitute for many a parent was the 80's / early 90's phase of the LCD (liquid crystal display) handheld game. I first came into contact with these games via my older brother who had a bizarre winged American football game, Astro Wars, and Space Invaders. I didn't really understand what was going on but seeing the bright lights and hearing the blips was fascinating.

I don't remember who got it for me, but the sea-change game was a TomyTronic. For anyone who hasn't ever seen these they are the perfect embodiment of the 1980's; a handheld game that you look through a viewfinder to experience beautifully crisp wireframe 3D. Like a colour Vectrex if you will, yet it uses the sunlight at the top of the machine and 4 x AA batteries of course! Everything had batteries in the 80's and I always had a pack on the go! So after collecting the TomyTronics I became obsessed and asked for LCD games for any Birthday or Christmas.

Like most kids in the late 80's the Teenage Mutant Ninja Turtles were the craze of the time. I collected the bubble gum cards, the comics, the merchandise, the toys, and it was my first film I chose to go and see. So it was obvious that I would have the LCD game from Konami. It's a beautiful shape, a perfect turtle green and the actual game itself may be primitive but it's addictive. Everything plays out on one screen and is perfect for car journeys and sofa sitting before the GameBoy graced us.

Another fantastic series was Nintendo's Game & Watch. I had the blue Super Mario Bros, Mario Factory, Mario 3 and Tetris wrist watches. Of course, the acquisition of the watches made me very popular in the playground, but constantly taking it off to show people became a problem. It did mean I could play Super Mario 3 whilst at school, which gives me a few Dennis the Menace points. Still, my favourite watch of all time though is my James Bond 007 black watch...if ya askin!

Tiger Electronics made a huge range of LCD games to cash in on various franchises and being obsessed with Golden Axe I had to have the game. I think I may have had Sonic the Hedgehog and Paperboy as well.

The Argos catalogue was the resource for most household goods in the 1980's and the LCD game was no different. When you went round to most people's houses they had similar stuff in their homes to you and it either came from Argos or their late rival Index. Everybody shopped there which seems bizarre now as their business model hasn't actually changed and I'm surprised they are still around! I do have fond memories of the Argos catalogue though and It was my first job apart from a paperboy; it seems chucking papers into people's gardens like in the game is frowned upon.

To quote Bill Bailey though, it really was the 'laminated book of dreams' and that's where most kids would drool over computers, consoles, and LCD games. The LCD game is now an icon of the period and of course the start of gaming on the go. I wonder what an 8-year-old me would think of a Nintendo 3DS, maybe that would cause some Dr Who style rift in time.

DONKEY KONG COUNTRY

Silicon. Rendered. Models. Three words. I didn't entirely understand what they meant, but I was sure it meant more *"better'er!"*

We first saw the model renders in the magazines, the gorgeous 3 dimensional monkey characters and the stylised feel of the first level jungle. We were drip fed screenshots and hype surrounding what was going to become the most beautiful looking platformer in its era. I was fascinated with silicon rendered sprites and found the idea of pre-rendering graphics on a workstation and scaling them into 16bit technology very intriguing. It was a buzz phrase from then on used in magazines and conversations with friends...

"Is the game using Silicon Rendering?"
"I hope so!"

Everybody's interest was being pulled by the shiny new leap forward into 32bit 3D gaming. The 5th generation was upon us and our 16bit machines were pumping out the very best you could possibly squeeze out of 16bits. They were in their prime and after various expansions plugged in, chips squished into cartridges, and ram forced into chipboards I thought I'd seen the best of the 16bit world in titles such as Dynamite Heady, Starfox, Virtua Racing and the like.

In November 1994 I was well and truly immersed in the console gaming world. I was a Sega Megadrive 2 owner looking forward to the 32X, however having access to a SNES via a best friend meant I always kept abreast of Nintendo developments (and read his Super Play magazine... he kept those magazines in pristine condition!) He always had the new consoles and games as well, so I was in good stead to get to play the game first around its winter release. I had just turned 14 and was in an embryonic stage starting my transition from gamer geek to musician...well... geek! I was captain of the school basketball team, listening to Oasis and Nirvana unplugged, interested in girls and starting to go out late wandering the streets with 'the lads' and just being generally cheeky and active.

So, why is this personal nod relevant? Well this game symbolises the end of an era to me. Not in a sad way as I enjoyed gaming after this time but just not in such an innocent way. As soon as the world started to reveal itself to me in my teens I looked at things differently. My attention was pulled in different directions such as my first cigarette, the sound of that guitar solo, how song lyrics spoke to me, the colour of the lipstick that girl I liked wore and all that complicated white noise fuzz that enters your head around that age.

Donkey Kong Country signifies the last massive release that I enjoyed free of the self-awareness of trying to 'fit in' in some way. An untainted naivety that can only come with innocence and purity. That all went very soon around this period and in time I'd be learning guitar, had a 'proper' girlfriend, and was listening to Britpop whilst high on a badly rolled spliff; you don't really come back from that and that childlike wonder kind of dies with it.

I believe this is something which I think I'm tapping into by being obsessed with retro gaming today. I think we are all trying to recreate that emotion of being a child within. That particular period in gaming and 85 - 96 was the golden time for me and I'm sure the younger generation will take the PS2 and upwards to heart in the same way I do the C64 and Megadrive. Some a little older than me tend to argue that when games crossed over into the mainstream the independent side of the business died too, so to them the party was already over I guess…

Anyway, this game is the perfect platform game for me. The mist covered mines, snow blizzards that got progressively worse, lighting techniques to display depth and space and animation that adds soul and character as well as personality. It really was an incredible job from game company RARE who obviously went on to create some of the best games in history. The game had so much hype and its development was covered in the press so intensely that you couldn't fail to miss it. The magazines covered it month by month in the run up to the winter holiday season as it was going to be Nintendo's big release.

Now, if you've been paying attention you'll realise I didn't have a SNES, but I was so excited about this release I bought multi-format magazines such as Edge around the time just to get glimpses of what I'd inevitably be playing round my friend's house! Ice caves, the infamous mine-cart levels (which I liked and I've never met anyone else who does!), boss battles with huge sprites and of course the audio. The music and audio in this game is nothing short of phenomenal and really shows what you can do with the SNES sound architecture. The sonics reacted to the environment such as reverb and echo, the baddies had their own sonic tag, and everything seemed to draw you further into its world. People remember the soundtracks to this game still today and much like Mario have stood the test of time as great pieces in their own right. The Kong family reminded me of a similar vibe to the Dizzy family back in the day and the advent of riding on the different animals to the Yoshi mechanic expanded it further. There were things to collect, secrets to find, and so much more that I'm sure most of you reading this know all too well.

It's the last hurrah of Nintendo's greatest home console and a game that made a generation of gamers not migrate to PlayStation just yet... this didn't last of course. I still play this game today on my GameBoy Advance before I go to sleep. This along with the Supermario games reminds me of the peak of console gaming before CDs and cartridges were something you blew on before play. I haven't met many people who don't like it and although there may be some who don't, they can't deny its fantastic graphic and audio achievements; even if they don't like the gameplay. I may be older now but like the art of a great artist, musician, film, or TV programme, we'll always have the games and Nintendo definitely know how to make a classic. Nintendo, we salute you. Thank you.

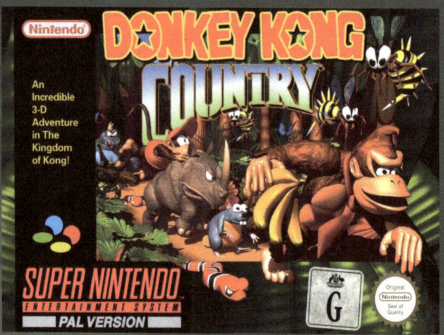

MEMORIES OF...

ARCADES & CRASHING WAVES

A bowling alley has such a nostalgic smell for me... people say it's the smell of the oil they use to coat the lanes. As soon as you open the doors to the complex all the stimuli hit you at once like time travel. The bright 50's style neon lights, coins dropping from machines, the clang of a table ice hockey puck, a cheering crowd as a strike hits home, the familiar colour scheme of the maple and pine and of course the arcade machines.

I was brought up in a town called Havant in Hampshire, so being by the sea I had my fair share of arcade experiences from neighbouring seaside towns and their piers such as Portsmouth, Brighton, Bournemouth and nearby Hayling Island. I played the Sega 80's classics such as Afterburner, Outrun, Space Harrier, A.B.Cop, Super Hang On, Powerdrift and the like. I always pestered my Dad for a few quid whenever we were near one.

There's a magic to an arcade cabinet. I can't say I'd take it over a home experience where you can relax surrounded by creature comforts, but there is something about a stand-alone game machine and a group of you crowded round a cabinet whilst you try not to buckle under the pressure. Gawping at the graphic design and sitting in a beautifully made racing seat as you completely immerse yourself in pixels can have a lasting effect on the imagination of an 8 year old boy as let's face it... it was normally 3 mins max as the machines were rigged rock solid to take your coins!

Most of my arcade experiences as a young kid were captivating, inspiring but also solitary. It wasn't until I started going to my local swimming baths with a few friends that I really experienced the full excitement of arcade cabs. This is mainly due to one cab that caught our attention; Golden Axe. I'm sure you don't need me to elaborate much on Golden Axe as it rightly claims legendary status. Although its aged in a clunky manner and the franchise has kind of been battered, those memories of playing the game will last forever. The swimming baths also had other games such as Gauntlet, The Simpsons, Teenage Mutant Ninja Turtles (The Arcade Game) and Wrestlefest. Naturally we had little pocket money, so anyone who had a couple of quid on them was a man of great riches!

By 1991 the Megadrive was releasing arcade ports of Sega classics like Alien Syndrome and Splatterhouse meaning that it wasn't until the early 90's new-wave of arcade machines came in that I was truly captivated. After a holiday with a late friend of mine Chris Jackson (where we spent what money we could playing Virtua Fighter) I became interested in the next-gen arcade boards and this is where my local bowling alley comes in.

AMF Bowling Alley in Bedhampton was where I went to play the new big hitters with friends. I loved bowling anyway and used to go for birthday parties and in the holidays. The environment was something I was drawn to having a penchant for the American 50's & 60's style and in my local alley they had a very small section at the end of the building for arcade cabs, which luckily for me, always seemed up-to-date with the new titles. I'll never forget playing Ridge Racer there for the first time as well as playing such classics as Sega Rally, Daytona, Virtua Racing, Virtua Fighter 1 & 2, and House Of The Dead 1 & 2.

Nintendo/Rare were using the arcade games Killer Instinct & Crusin USA to allegedly show off their up-coming system - Ultra 64 - which was released as the N64 in the UK. Playing these silicon rendered gems at the bowling alley really made you feel you were immersed in the newest technology, alongside Donkey Kong Country which made RARE the company to watch! Anyway, next-gen technology was here and it cost a quid each time! I normally only went down with a fiver so I had to choose wisely. There's something about an arcade racer for me... Ridge Racer, Daytona, Sega Rally, Crazy Taxi, Virtua Racing... It doesn't get much better than that line-up.

MEMORIES OF...
BRING YA FRIENDS!

We all like a list so after the article on arcades I thought It appropriate to list some of my favourite multiplayer games. Gaming with two is always a catalyst for laughter, which is the best antidote to anything.

NBA JAM Tournament Edition - 32X
Mortal Kombat 2 - 32X
Motocross Championship - 32X
Virtua Fighter - 32X

Micro Machines Turbo Tournament - Megadrive
Sonic 2 - Megadrive
FIFA International Soccer - Megadrive
EA Hockey - Megadrive
Street Racer - Megadrive
Virtua Racing - Megadrive
Streets Of Rage 3 - Megadrive
Sensible Soccer - Megadrive
NBA Live 95 - Megadrive

Street Fighter 2 - SNES
Mario Kart - SNES
Donkey Kong Country - SNES
Zombies Ate My Neighbours - SNES

Super Mario Bros - NES

Goldeneye - N64
Mario Kart - N64
Wave Race - N64
Super Smash Bros - N64
V-Rally - N64

Daytona - Arcade
Killer Instinct - Arcade
House Of The Dead - Arcade
Gauntlet - Arcade
Virtua Cop - Arcade

Bruce Lee - C64
Rodland - C64
IK+ - C64
Speedball 2 - C64/Amiga

Doom (Deathmatch) - PC

SEGA SATURN

The next generation was upon us in 94-95. I tend to reminisce about that period a lot as it's a subject close to my heart. Gaming had reached a cross-over peak having showed itself to be an extremely lucrative business. The world and his wife wanted a piece of the action: Amiga 32, Sega 32X, Sega Saturn, Atari Jaguar, Panasonic 3DO, Phillips CDi, Sony Playstion, Neo Geo CD, NEC not to mention Nintendo's N64 in the distance - it was never ending! I would pour over magazines for any information and the race to release was a buzz! My friends were obsessed too. Many debates would start up about the benefits of each machine and I began to buy multi-format next-gen themed magazines like Ultimate Future Games and Edge to get information.

Then the time we had all been waiting for struck and every console was out of my price range.

One friend bought a 3DO and another a Sony Playstation. Our friendship group had no Jaguars, no Amiga 32s and definitely no Saturns. I had a 32X and an obsession with Oasis and Britpop that was starting to consume me completely. One day I fished out an old beaten up nylon strung acoustic that was in the cupboard (my Sisters from a decade previous - she didn't even learn) and mastered my first few chords. As soon as I started learning Oasis songs I started writing my own and before long instead of learning I was composing. They may have been cliché and rubbish but I was away. From there I went onto other musical styles and song-writing such as Neil Young, My Vitriol and Jeff Buckley. I then joined a band in the late 90's and music became my lifeline, my safety net, expression, creative outlet and life choice.

My point is this, I missed the 5th generation stand-alone consoles as I was so busy learning guitar. I never owned a Playstation or a Saturn and I didn't even get an N64 until 2001. So, even though I still played games it meant that the big expectation and excitement was never met in its full capacity in the 5th generation as I was all about the Rock & Roll from 1995!

Having been a Sega owner in the Megadrive 2 for a long time and even investing in the 32X idea, I always had a soft spot for the Saturn; especially as it immediately became the underdog against the Playstation. The games seemed to appeal to me more and the arcade ports of Sega classics and the exclusives for the system seemed bizarre and different. The N64 took over though, becoming the party console of choice at my friends' houses and the Saturn was left behind in my thoughts being replaced by smoky clubs, Marshall amps, pubs and guitars. So as you can see, I've had periods in my life where I've lost my obsession for retro games but it will always come back to me like a guiding lighthouse on a dark misty night.

Some years back, I rekindled my retro game fascination and the Sega Saturn was something I instantly pursued. It was a great surprise that my partner bought me a Sega Saturn mk2 as a Christmas present knowing that it was something I wanted to get to fill in that piece of retro history that I couldn't afford at the time. She even got me two games to play on Christmas Day: Alien Trilogy and Manx TT.

It was an incredibly thoughtful gift and she even managed to get it in its original box with a manual. I'm not collecting in the hording sense at all as I sell games to get ones I really want to play but I am searching for gems which has been, and continues to be, an incredibly pleasurable and geeky experience. I've fallen in love with the machine: its looks, the clunky technology, the pad, the games and its chequered history. I adore everything about it and some of the games I have such as Nights, Sega Rally, Clockwork Knight 2, Manx TT, Rayman, Virtua Fighter 2 and Daytona (and the Championship Circuit Edition) have been my first time playing them on a Saturn, so I'm only just experiencing them… this is discovery like its 1995!

The Saturn has become my main gaming system, like an old friend that you want to go round and visit after a long day, or just to ride around in the car with listening to "Dayeeeetoooooonnna!". Sometimes the discs need a clean, the boxes are always creased and dog-eared because they are made of cardboard and the joy pad cable is chunky and never stays straight. But it's these things along with the opening jingle and triangular polygons flashing across the screen that define the reign of the Saturn and Sega's 32bit era.

My Saturn sits under my TV and I am proud that it has been rescued to be used as it was meant to be used… in short bursts of arcade joy!

As I've said, I've become a little obsessed with this era in gaming history and particularly Sega's 32bit era as that was my focus as a kid. Tom Kalinske (the CEO of Sega in the early 90's to 96) is a fascinating man and there are many interviews with him out there to listen to. Researching the period is a fractured and somewhat misty experience. There seems to be so many conflicting stories, biased data and communication breakdowns that to get to the truth of what was happening between Sega of Japan and America is a Sherlock episode in itself (and one which I wouldn't feel confident talking about here in any detail). That's for the big boys like the Console Wars book and the like!

Obviously what is true is the facts. And we know that Sony, after being turned down by both Sega and Nintendo, went it alone and took pole position in the video game market. That in itself is an incredible achievement which was unexpected and bizarre! Not quite as exciting as Sega taking the market share from Nintendo but still fantastic. For me though, Sony has never had the same character as the two early nineties titans Sega and Nintendo. I loved my PS2 but it will never be the same feeling as that Sega logo in blue and white followed by the AM2 palm tree… arcade fun is a loading time away!

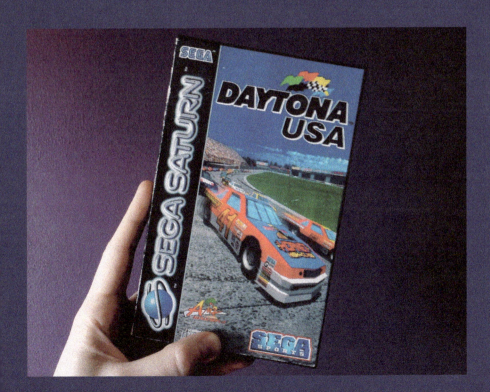

PANIC ATTACKS & RETRO LIFE HACKS

The doors of the tube train slide shut and that electric motor whirs quickly into life as you're catapulted forward violently from the station. You manage to get a seat as you came from Hanger Lane on the far West of London, but the tube is now completely rammed from White City....

Shortened breath, sweating, nausea, spinning head, tightness in your chest... TICK TOCK TICK TOCK... You've been fighting it ever since you stepped on to the tube but now it's breaking out and every stop is the next stop you're going to get off but you keep telling yourself to try and ride it out; literally! But everything starts melting like a Dali painting and you fear this could be a blackout for you...

Wait! This is a bit heavy, isn't it? For a light read!

I was simply trying to put you in the picture of a brief and unfortunate time in my life when I lived and worked in central London. I was flirting with celebrity culture through employment as a runner for an Audio Post Production house; working on Top Of The Pops (before it died), Later With Jools Holland and a few other audio places in Soho. I suffered from Panic Attacks and it was starting to cripple my everyday life and working in one of the busiest cities in the world didn't help one bit... Until the advent of one tiny clam shell designed retro diamond that came in a cobalt blue colour; the Nintendo GameBoy Advance SP.

The Nintendo GameBoy Advance SP was quite literally my saviour. So much so, that I carried it everywhere and anywhere I was going just in case I felt the small electric pulses that signal the start of a panic episode. When I deployed operation GameBoy SP I'd be transported into the gaming world where I tricked myself into thinking I was safe and it worked EVERY time.

My girlfriend back then brought it for me after me being obsessed with it for a long time before its launch. I never had an original one but the backlit clamshell version particularly appealed to my clumsy nature and its smaller and light friendly design was a no-brainer. I remember its day of purchase so clearly. We hopped onto the 83 bus to Wembley and I also remember not being allowed it that day because "it isn't your birthday just yet!". I can honestly say it was the most excited I'd been about any gaming media since being a kid. I hadn't got a console in the same year of launch for many a year and even though I was 23, I felt like a kid again.

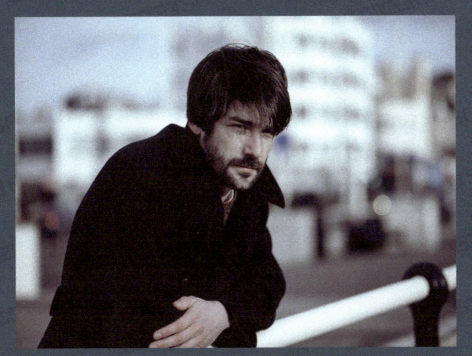

Within the pack I got Lord Of The Rings - Two Towers (as obviously the films where coming out around this period and I loved them), Donkey Kong Country, Mario Kart Super Circuit and Doom 2. I started collecting games wherever I saw a second hand shop, as you could pick up games for a couple of quid then. I was Nintendo mad around this period as being a latecomer to the N64 I was again picking carts up for £3 - £5 and building a little collection; not as easy nowadays!

This little victory over my panic attacks is a testament to gaming as it is a perfect anecdote explaining that thing we call escapism. Today, to me, there are gamers who only communicate via a headset on Call Of Duty and World of Warcraft, then there's gamers who only play Fifa but still weigh in on console arguments and then there's people who spend their time hating on the opposite brand that they have, probably more than actually playing the games! Then there's us. The sentimental childlike dream-heads that love the emotion of playing a simple game; that engagement in an otherwise lost moment. It can conquer any fear or self-doubt and help you forget about your worries and your strife (to quote Baloo Bear from Jungle Book!).

I believe that whatever type of gamer you are, it's all about escapism. For me the retro side of gaming is a time capsule. I experience all those fond and safe-feeling childhood emotions again and again every time I turn the power button on.

Continue?...

THANKS...

The RGDS Podcast, Andy Godoy, Aaron (Walking Stick) White, Garron (The Brain In A Jar), Benny (The Bear), Jon (Blue Pants), Games You Loved, Neil Grayson, The Twitter Retro Gaming community.

All photography and old archive photos owned by me or otherwise stated
Cover photo by **www.aaron-bennett.format.com**

I have tried to credit where due the very few sourced photos and box scans where I could, but apologies if I have not been able to find the original owner.

All product and company names are trademarks™ or registered® trademarks of their respective holders. Use of them does not imply any affiliation with or endorsement by them.
**Sega, Nintendo, Commodore, Sinclair, Amstrad, 32X
Gameboy, Tiger, Dizzy, Rare, Ocean, AM2, AMF, Sega Saturn**
are trademarks or registered trademarks and I am in no way affiliated with any of them, any offence caused by use of any logo is not intended.

Flimbos Quest screen grab
https://www.youtube.com/watch?v=0msxihp1fFQ

Dizzy screen grabs
http://www.8-bitcentral.com/blog/2015/dizzy.html

Sega Saturn photo
Wikipedia

Virtua Racing screen grab
https://www.youtube.com/watch?v=RG-aQL9SoAA

Jte Pack screen grab
http://gamesdbase.com/Media/SYSTEM/Sinclair_ZX_Spectrum/Snap/big/Jetpac_-_1983_-_Ultimate_-_Play_the_Game.jpg

Mortal Kombat 2 advert
http://www.retrogamingaus.com/wordpress/wp-content/uploads/2012/01/Mortal-Kombat-II-32X.jpg

Donkey Kong Country & Mario Land screen grabs
http://nintendo.wikia.com/ - https://www.youtube.com/watch?v=ziPX5JZa_FY
&
http://images.nintendolife.com/news/2014/02/month_of_kong_the_making_of_donkey_kong_country/attachment/3/original.jpg

32X Adverts
https://s-media-cache-ak0.pinimg.com/736x/9c/97/6b/9c976b189824c2ef8621db2884e97064.jpg
http://socksmakepeoplesexy.net/images/irish/32x-print.jpg
http://socksmakepeoplesexy.net/index.php?a=irish-ads2
https://www.pinterest.com/pin/396316835937647934/

Front cover Speech bubble
<a href="http://www.freepik.com/free-vector/hand-drawn-bubbles-speech_764271.htm">Designed by Freepik</a>

Other sourced pics have web address in them if not my own

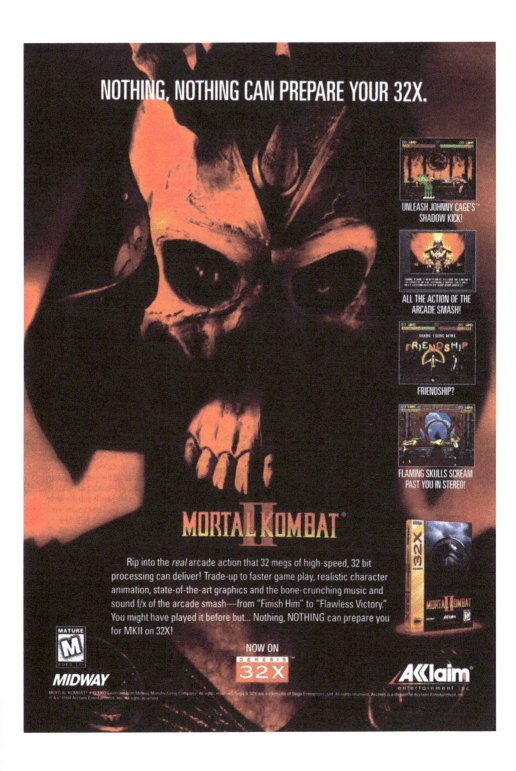